BIZARRE BODIES

by Robin Twiddy

Minneapolis, Minnesota

CREDITS

Images are courtesy of Shutterstock.com. With thanks to Getty Images, Thinkstock Photo, and iStockphoto.

Recurring images – pics five (paper), Sonechko57 (splats), sebastian ignacio coll (explosion), MoonRock (texture), Ilija Erceg (eyes), Amy Li (illustrations). Cover – svtdesign, engagestock, mary_stocker, PannaKotta. 2–3 – Evgenia Zhilyakova, Zurijeta. 4–5 – svtdesign, Mooi Design, Sunspire, Elnur, Alena Razumova. 6–7 – svtdesign, Anatolir, ivanvislov, Sklo Studio. 8–9 – Krakenimages.com, vitstudio, wowomnom. 10–11 – Giulio_Fornasar, ProStockStudio. 12–13 – Baksiabat, CREATISTA, SewCream. 14–15 – WhiteDragon, Jacek Chabraszewski, africa_pink. 16–17 – Prostock-studio, Gelpi. 18–19 – Oxy_gen, Fertas. 20–21 – 9nong, Amanita Silvicora, paper_Owl. 22–23 – Sujono sujono, Iryna Kuznetsova, VectorPlotnikoff. 24–25 – Prostock-studio, Yellow Cat. 26–27 – bioraven, hudzaqwan, Ihor Bulyhin. 28–29 – Robert Kneschke, Alena Razumova, Sudowoodo. 30 – Syda Productions.

Library of Congress Cataloging-in-Publication Data is available at www.loc.gov or upon request from the publisher.

ISBN: 979-8-88822-017-7 (hardcover)
ISBN: 979-8-88822-205-8 (paperback)
ISBN: 979-8-88822-332-1 (ebook)

© 2024 Booklife Publishing
This edition is published by arrangement with Booklife Publishing.

North American adaptations © 2024 Bearport Publishing Company. All rights reserved. No part of this publication may be reproduced in whole or in part, stored in any retrieval system, or transmitted in any form or by any means, electronic, mechanical, photocopying, recording, or otherwise, without written permission from the publisher.

For more information, write to Bearport Publishing, 5357 Penn Avenue South, Minneapolis, MN 55419.

CONTENTS

Serious Science 4
Roller Coaster Rumble 6
The Speed of Thought 8
Super Strength 10
Hold Your Breath 12
New You 14
Is That My Body? 16
Freaky Fingernails 18
How Many Hiccups? 20
Rapunzel, Rapunzel 22
Pinkie Power 24
The Taste of Music 26
Totally Silly 28
Glossary 31
Index 32
Read More 32
Learn More Online 32

SERIOUS SCIENCE

Science is always serious, right? Wrong! Science can be anything but stuffy and stiff.

Bodies are far from serious. And the science in them can be sillier than you think.

Welcome to the Silly Zone. Get ready to learn the strangest things about bodies!

ROLLER COASTER RUMBLE

Have you ever been on a roller coaster with a big hill? When the coaster finally drops, it feels like your stomach is sinking.

You might get the same feeling in a car that goes over a hill too fast. Why?

Normally, everything inside your body is pulled down by **gravity**. But when you drop suddenly, it's like your insides become weightless.

There is less **force** pulling your insides down. This gives you the feeling in your stomach.

THE SPEED OF THOUGHT

Wiggle your leg. Now, stick your tongue out. Your body moves as soon as you want it to, right?

Nope! There is a very short time between when you think about moving and when your body actually moves.

When you want to move, your brain sends a message through your body.

Some messages take longer. You can stick out your tongue faster than you can wiggle your leg. That's because your tongue is closer to your brain!

SUPER STRENGTH

In 1982, Angela Cavallo's son was trapped under a car. She lifted the car to save him. Did Angela have superhuman strength?

Probably not. Scientists believe this sudden strength was caused by stress.

When a person is very scared, their body releases a **chemical**. It makes the body work harder and faster.

But this strength happens only when danger is real. So, scientists can't study it (unless they want to be supervillains)!

HOLD YOUR BREATH

How long can you hold your breath? In 2016, Aleix Segura held his breath for 24 minutes and 3 seconds!

Breathing is important. When you breathe in, you take in **oxygen**.

Our bodies need oxygen to stay alive. As bodies use oxygen, they make a waste gas called **carbon dioxide**. Breathing out gets rid of it.

Want to hold your breath for longer? Try going underwater! Your body slows down so it uses less oxygen below the surface.

NEW YOU

If the tires on your bike pop, you replace them. The same goes for your brakes.

Every part of the bike may be replaced. But if this happens, is it the same bike?

Your body is made up of tiny parts, too. They are called **cells**. Over time, cells die. New cells replace the old.

Fortunately, you are not like a bike. Some cells in your body last your entire life.

IS THAT MY BODY?

We like to think our brains are very clever. But it turns out they can be easy to trick.

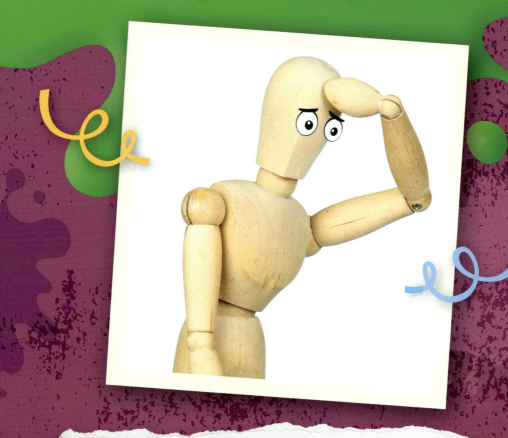

Scientists can make someone think their body is giant or tiny.

Scientists put people in a **virtual reality** game. In the game, the pictures of their bodies were replaced with others of very different sizes.

The people started to feel like the virtual bodies were their own!

FREAKY FINGERNAILS

Your fingernails are always growing. How long can they go?

One of the longest fingernails ever was grown by a man named Shridhar Chillal. His thumbnail was more than 77 inches (197 cm) long!

People once believed that nails kept growing even after death. But this isn't true.

When someone dies, the skin around their nails shrinks. This can make it look like the nails have grown.

HOW MANY HICCUPS?

Hic! When you have the hiccups, it can be hard to do basic things.

Hiccups happen when the muscle that helps you breathe is bothered. Suddenly, air is pulled into the throat. This makes the funny hiccup sound.

Hiccups usually go away after a while. But not for Charles Osborne.

Charles fell and knocked himself out. When he woke up, hiccups began. Charles had hiccups for the next 68 years!

RAPUNZEL, RAPUNZEL

Does it seem silly that Rapunzel had visitors climb up her hair?

Maybe it's not such a crazy idea. Human hair is almost as strong as steel.

A single strand of hair is strong enough to hold the weight of a deck of cards without breaking.

The average person has about 150,000 hairs. Together, they could hold the weight of two elephants.

PINKIE POWER

When it comes to strength, your hands have a little secret.

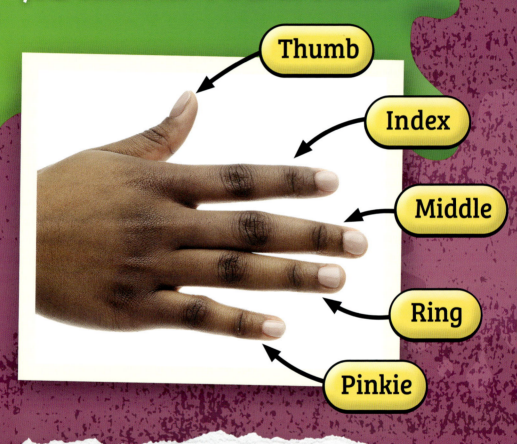

Most of the strength in your hand comes from your pinkie and ring fingers.

Scientists put hands to the test. First, they had people test their strength with all their fingers. Then, they did the test again without using the pinkie and ring fingers.

The hands were twice as strong using all fingers.

THE TASTE OF MUSIC

Some people have a condition called **synesthesia** (si-nuh-STEE-zhuh). Their brains mix up their senses.

There are different kinds of synesthesia. Some people see a color when they look at letters and numbers. Others get a taste in their mouth when they hear music.

Professor Simon Baron-Cohen discovered that this condition mixes up senses the same way every time.

In a test, he asked someone the colors of a group of letters and numbers. Later, the person gave the same colors.

TOTALLY SILLY

We have learned a lot about bodies.

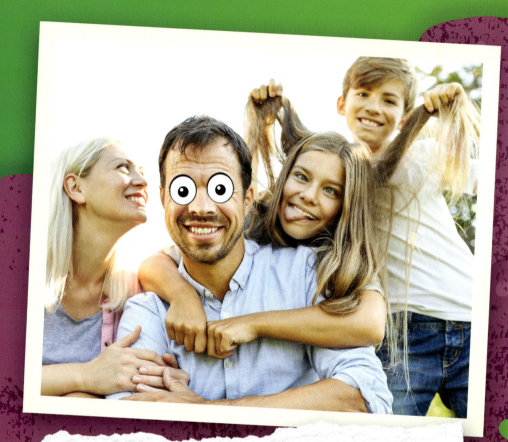

There were endless hiccups and superstrong hair. We also learned that fingernails can keep growing and growing!

Our bodies are silly from head to toe. But is there a point to all this silliness?

Silly

Also silly

Sillier

Really silly

Yes! We learn lots of useful things when we look at how silly our bodies can be!

We have a bunch of silly scientists to thank for the silly science. Silly scientists + silly bodies = serious science!

WHICH FACTS ABOUT BODIES ARE THE SILLIEST?

GLOSSARY

carbon dioxide a gas that people and animals breathe out

cells very tiny parts of all living things

chemical a natural or human-made substance

force a push or pull that causes movement

gravity the force that pulls all things on Earth toward the ground

oxygen a gas in the air that people and animals need to breathe

synesthesia a condition where using one of the senses makes the brain use another, unrelated sense at the same time

virtual reality a fake world made by computers that looks and sounds real

INDEX

brains 9, 16, 26
breathe 12–13, 20
cells 15
hair 22–23, 28
hiccup 20–21, 28
message 9
nails 18–19, 28
roller coaster 6–7
strength 10–11, 22–25, 28
synesthesia 26

READ MORE

Finan, Catherine C. *The Human Body (X-treme Facts: Science).* Minneapolis: Bearport Publishing Company, 2021.

Mason, Paul. *Hair-Raising Human Body Facts (Body Bits).* New York: Gareth Stevens Publishing, 2023.

LEARN MORE ONLINE

1. Go to **www.factsurfer.com** or scan the QR code below.
2. Enter "**Bizarre Bodies**" into the search box.
3. Click on the cover of this book to see a list of websites.